MW01592431

HEINZ 56

Poems by

Amanda Reynolds

MAIN STREET RAG PUBLISHING COMPANY
CHARLOTTE, NORTH CAROLINA

Cover photograph by Clyde Hare.
Author photo by: Rocky Raco Photography

Acknowledgments:

The author wishes to thank the following editors and journals where these
poems first appeared:

> *Gargoyle* : "Kurt Vonnegut Flunked Thermodynamics"
> *Gander Mountain Review:* "What the Train Says," "The Banana
>   Explosion of 1936," "The Shape of a City"
> *Mississippi Crow:* "Wishing You Were Here," "Bridge of Sighs"
> *Floyd County Moonshine:* "What a Choice Means"
> *Edifice Wrecked:* "What We Were Eating"
> *The Broken City:* "The Great Pittsburgh Fire (1845)"
> *Schuylkill Valley Journal:* "If This is the End," "A Woman is Worth
>   Twice that of a Man"

Library of Congress Control Number: 2011942434

ISBN: 978-1-59948-337-5

Produced in the United States of America

Main Street Rag
PO Box 690100
Charlotte, NC 28227
www.MainStreetRag.com

for my grandfather

CONTENTS

I have never been more in love
with smoke and dirt…

—Anthony Trollope on visiting Pittsburgh

WISHING YOU WERE HERE

You can laugh, but I'll take one look at ketchup
on your plate and tell you whether it's Heinz.
When Mom gave birth to me, her focal point
was outside the window, a giant Isaly's vitrolite sign,
and the Eat 'n Park commercials are my favorite thing
about Christmas. I missed more of Pittsburgh
than I thought. I was too young to know it,
but the PETA protestors were naked behind signs
they carried down Fifth Avenue, and I was lucky
I'd left the fur coat grandma bought me at home.

I missed a few other things too: Wiener World
in the cultural district sits right next to a porn
shop, and Kennedy in his maroon auto passing
Gus and YaYa's Icey Balls and double coated butter
popcorn on the North Side, which is one word or two,
whichever you'd like. I might have enjoyed field trips
to a baseball game had I known that in the parking lot
I could stand where Louis Bierbaur guarded second base
after being pirated from the Philadelphia Athletics.

Didn't everyone hate Three Rivers? How damn mod
were those weekend warriors who didn't realize
what they saw on stage in Brian Jones, soon-to-be member
of the 27 club. Even though Westview burned,
there's still Kennywood where each day two tons
of corndogs swirl around stomachs on the Jackrabbit,
and grease from the potato patch fries makes it hard
to hold onto the Thunderbolt's safety bar across your lap.
If someone tells you the park's open,
check your zipper. The coasters are faster after dark.

Please don't tell. I was the first generation born without a Pittsburgh zip code. Dear Saltsburg, half an hour east of all I wish I'd seen and done, I hated you every day.

I.

RED BELT

In the 1940's, an engineer, Joseph White, designed a system of roads to circumvent traffic around the congested downtown area in Pittsburgh. The roads form concentric rings around the city with the outermost being red, followed by orange, yellow, green, and blue. In 1995, a three mile purple belt was added downtown to highlight the city's attractions.

After you I dated a boy who flipped
a quarter to decide it all:
fish or chicken, red or blue,
to cheat or not to cheat.
But that's all too nonchalant
for me, so I choose the red belt,
largest and grandest first.
There's no Virgil guiding me,
but I rock the classics on DVE loud.

I start out thinking how I'd like
to marry someone like Pittsburgh's native
son, Mike Fink: "half horse
and half alligator" joked Davy Crockett.
But I'm only thinking this way
because you were in my dreams
last night again. Damn first loves. Damn you.
You, riding your bike eight miles
to my house when we were fifteen.
You, jumping from the roof of my dorm
with Mike in college. You and I, dancing
the night before I left for Florida.
Your living room spinning and us
in limbo. I'm driving to forget
you've found someone new. Driving

and thinking of Mike Fink
shooting whiskey glasses
from his woman's head and dragging
keelboats up the river.
Oh to be drunk and happy all day long.

Quickly, I realize it's a big joke.
These roads are too far from the city I love.
I need a map. The wind chill is fourteen
below, and the crossing guard
only comes out to help the cute kids across.
There's a dead deer outside the gunsmith's
shop, frozen creeks, corn fields,
and abandoned barns. It's too much like
where we grew up. Like when Barry
jumped through the fire and we ended
up at the hospital. When Tim took
you, Laura, and me four-wheeling up the coal piles
and we smacked into that tree. Hard.
When you and Autumn were caught
parked in the field and everyone heard
about it in school the next day.
What level of hell is that punishment?

I imagined how I'd stop for lunch
at a cute café, take pictures of old mills
and meet the "locals," but it's too damn cold
to get out of the car except for gas.
I spend thirteen dollars and eighty three cents
on a map I don't use. A black truck

Amanda Reynolds

follows me for miles, and all I can think
is how we drove for hours through back roads,
how I could drive to your house eyes closed.
I keep thinking how I shouldn't tell this story.

I just want to get back home, so I take 28
past Pittsburgh Mills. When I see
the Highland Park Bridge it starts to feel better.
At the Veterans Bridge exit I'm really feeling good.
The city sits frozen and wedged in the rivers.
My new house you've never seen waits upon the hill.
It's five days until Christmas and the sight of
the cold tall buildings feels safe and good.
Can you replace the love of a man
with the love of a place? I'll be alright tonight.

THE MOLLY MAGUIRES

There's one thing I'll tell you and don't you forget
That your back with the droppers is all wringing wet,
Your clothes they are soaking; your shoes are wet through,
Oh! Never be a miner whatever you do. (Miner's Song)

The Molly Maguires didn't exist,
but they killed
my great aunt's husband.
That's the family folklore.
The real Molly was in Ireland
organizing against the English,
or perhaps it was only men
dressed as meek women
striking the landowners down.
No such group claimed a love
for the city of Pittsburgh.
Accidents will happen,
says one mine owner,
in all great works.
No one is certain when he leaves home
for the pit mouth
about returning alive,
but the women here worry more than most.
The big bosses branded
the labor leaders: assassins,
incendiaries, thieves and gamblers.
Life itself was the gamble
working in mines in 1860.
The young boys
from dawn until dusk sucked
cold air through an open window,
picking and picking their lives away.

Amanda Reynolds

Their little spines curved
under old shawls, and they dropped handmade
mittens in a little miner's graveyard
beside the church bearing names
of many under ten.
Boys learned what matters:
the difference between slate and coal.
If they survived
the blasting and the collapsing walls,
they might have watched
the accused leaders hanged
at Pottsville in June
or seen fifteen hundred miners
lay down their tools
in July. And through
it all, a watchman called every hour
to keep the city working.

THE CITY OF PITTSBURGH WRITES TO VENICE

I've got more bridges you know. Four hundred
and forty-six on a good day, but who's counting?
And yes, we are real Italians:
ask Jimmy and Nino Sunseri down at the Strip.
The Stamoolis Brothers, Deluca's, and Penn Mac
have enough cheese and sfogliatelle for everyone.

Sure, you can brag all you want about canals,
but try and show me a hundred-pound
catfish sliced open with a man's boot inside.
We've got those in our rivers too.
From what I hear, only flies love your little streams
that smell worse than Philly cheesesteaks.

I admit, *Venezia* sounds beautiful in Italian,
but I'll cook your risotto for a year if you
can pronounce: Monongahela,
Wierton, Yoghiogheny, Duquesne,
Versailles, Beltzhoover, and Wilmerding
without cracking up. Go ahead and try it.

Yeah, we've got a regatta. With our boats
you don't even have to row. You're older,
but is that really something to brag about?
Napoleon, Attila, and the Crusades did so much
for your reputation, wouldn't you say?
You can even feed our pigeons without a license.

Amanda Reynolds

Stephen Foster could play Vivaldi under the *compo,*
and we've got plenty of room to die
while you're cramming bodies into San Michele
digging them up every 12 years to dump
them in a boneyard. City of Light did you say?
Queen of the Adriatic? *Serenissima?*

You're so proud of that printing press,
but what else? Try our banana split.
The first game of Bingo was played here,
the first emoticon typed, radio broadcasted,
ferris wheel conquered, and gas station built.
For god sakes, we made the first Big Mac!

Sure, once or twice we've had floods
like back in '36 when the water rose
46 feet and sank the streetcars,
but in case you haven't heard—you're drowning.
Send us a postcard, will you? We'd love to hear
from the most beautiful city under the sea.

FOR THE FEMALE FALCON ATOP
THE GULF BUILDING

Since last night I've watched online
the live camera feed of your nest.
It was ninety degrees here in Florida,
and I followed seagull tracks
on the beach, exotic delicacies for a peregrine.
The Pittsburgh pigeons you feast
on must be chewy or thick
like molten steel,
but I guess you like hard work.

I miss your city and the weather guide,
which sits on top of forty-four stories,
with its lantern that blinks
blue for rain or snow.

You have come and gone
some fifty-two times,
which is miraculously strange
considering the speckled garnet egg
that has appeared today,
direct center in the gravel
under a cold shadow. Still you haven't rested,
traveling out the limestone branches
of the skyscraper and back,
out and back, out and back.

Amanda Reynolds

Where is your mate?
You both watch over this city.
How long will you wait for him?
It is your resolution,
your love of Penn Plaza,
and the way you enjoy a slanderous perch
on the great statues we build to cover up
the damages we've done to the hills and valleys,
that keeps you returning to these stones.

It's not easy to stay so still. Trust me on this.
But how could you understand? The air pressure
from your two-hundred mile per hour
hunting dive would burst any ordinary bird's
lungs. The baffles in your nostrils
slow the wind velocity, and you are free to breathe.
What then for me? What love
could bring me back to a familiar place?

WHAT WE WERE EATING

When we leave Florida to visit Pittsburgh
and family for Christmas,
it's all about Iron City beer and Primanti Brothers—
grilled meat, chilled coleslaw, hot fried egg,
tomato, french fries, and lettuce all between slices
of thick chewy Italian bread. The same cook
flipped the pastrami last year, and you tell me
there isn't enough salt.
                    Imagine my Nanna
running the numbers and peddling penny stocks
to the neighbor women when things were slow,
and someone mentioned something great
and depressing all at once.
She'd leave Forbes Field with her second husband
(or was it the third?) when the Pirates beat
the Dodgers and everyone feasted
on warm baked beans, Klondikes, and skyscraper cones,
a nickel each. George Krohe wasn't yet the president
of chipped chopped ham. You've never heard
of chipped ham, like I don't know about jimmies
or pork rolls. But I promise if I had known,
I'd never have eaten any of it. It's all tofu and granola
for me
          now that I know there's pork lard
in the Gibble's chips. For 59 cents a pound
my ancestors bought hog legs shaped like footballs,
passed through a slow system of mechanized
preparation:
          the fat and muscle trimmings
collected and tumbled to separate the protein,

the meat reshaped, the adding of seasoning,
and the resulting flesh-colored pudding.
The paper-lined can molded the meat into
a loaf. After cooking for 5 ½ hours,
the result is 17 percent fat.
                              That's just how things turn out.
My grandmother learned from Isaly's
to cook an egg in the center of a meatloaf.
And you should have been there the day
she tried a pickle instead,
                              juice soaking into the cheddar
and meat, and everything covered in thick baked Heinz.
But tonight it's all about Primanti's on the Strip
and a hockey game. We'll have nachos later
because the cameraman likes blondes,
hat tricks, and nachos. I think there's something
I've forgotten about this place.
                              Maybe someone.
Something about the last goalie to face a puck
here without a mask. Something about
the silverware the Primanti uncles didn't order
for the dockworkers in the middle of the night
when they opened the doors to their restaurant
and how no one wanted to wait, so they piled
it all onto the bread in layers hot and cold.
Something about my grandma's pierogi recipe.
But you've got my knee under your warm palm
there's a white frost outside, and Crosby's got the puck.

Heinz 56

MOVING TO PITTSBURGH ALONE

The woman at the salon
was your dream girl,
thin and oily like angel hair
pasta, your one and only specialty.
As she leaned over the sink
and scraped shampoo hard
into my scalp, my eyes
slid back and forth
inches from hip bones,
your favorite body part on a girl,
the closest thing to licking a corpse
you could get.
Anyone would have noticed
the black lace inching just over
the designer denim, icing on the cake.
I think you could overlook
her tattoos, the way you nibbled
around mine. Looking up,
I wondered about silicone
as an artificial
flavor. As she sheared
off the dead ends I still
hate to lose, I watched
her back in the mirror, shoulder
bones like chicken wings,
and thought of your record,
gaining 11 pounds in one evening,
carcass by carcass, a piece of celery
here and there for the sake of blue cheese.
My new fridge will be full of tofu

Amanda Reynolds

and skim milk, strawberries,
spinach, and organic wines.
When she dried my hair,
she pulled me toward her
firm and strong—
nothing at all like you.

II.

ORANGE BELT

I was driving and downing
a B-vitamin smoothie behind
a dump truck spewing
exhaust fumes through my air vents
the third time I tried to find my way
around the 109-mile orange belt.
It's fitting. I'm a vegetarian
in a meat and potato city.
Country girl with a heroin-addict
neighbor in a new city home.
I hadn't yet abandoned all hope,
but I expected to be punished
for my crimes: a lie here or a hamburger there.
And half way along this day's path
I was ready to throw it all to the wolves.
There just *was* no sign.
Right, left, five-way intersection,
roundabout, up the hill or down.
No sign saying where to go from here.

Every time I get turned around and lost,
it all winds back to everything I'm looking for.
It's the holidays again, and I'm thinking how
when we were sixteen the diamond
you gave me was a quarter karat. At twenty,
with a full karat in hand, you promised to make
it four times bigger every four years.
This Christmas, without my 16-karat diamond,
I'm on my way to a holiday dinner alone
and find myself on the Orange Belt by accident,
I guess I'll follow this path as far as I can.
There's still hope, like that ring
in my armoire drawer I never open.

WAR SCENES

for Edward Jackson

I'm glad there are no bluebirds at the cliffs of Dover.
The mere idea of music as you were lured into the chalk
and flint of the coccoliths, is almost too much to bear.

Your bomber skimmed the earth's vertical crust
at the last second, and you knew that London was close
and safe for the moment.   France waited behind.

As a nose gunner, you spent hours in the turret
and once watched a cardboard box of Christmas tinsel
shred from a Heinkel 45 toward your wings.

Glitter caught the sun, leaving rainbows around the clouds.
The metal threw your radar into a tailspin
while the cardboard crashed straight through the turret.

I can't match now the black and white pictures of you,
with a movie star chin, riding the Allegheny in the *Rambler*
with the stinging frostbite from the hours you were trapped.

In London I was lost in Kensington within an hour.
You spent days shrugged down in your leather bomber
looking for relatives. Was London ever small?

After you returned to J&L to direct the barges
down the rivers, a B-25 ditched into the Monongahela.
Were you outside when the six men flew into the river?

Did you see only four men come back up from the icy
waters? I've heard people say in the bottom of the lochs
there are giant catfish as large as a man.

They say the plane carried an atomic bomb,
nuclear weapons, Mafia money, or Howard Hughes.
Soldiers closed off the banks and stole it away.

Do you know that to this day it's never been found?
I think you must have walked to the river that day
and squinted through the sun toward Bird's landing.

You might have imagined again the white cliffs,
the calm sea, the full tide, England glimmering and vast.
Listen! I too have heard music from these waters.

WHAT A CHOICE MEANS

She could have had suitors spread out
over the entire city—My great grandmother
would have turned Andrew Carnegie's
billion-dollar head. A young widow with
snowy hair, she lit Hazelwood afire
like St. Philomena's cast iron spires
and 225-foot tower, flames and sparks
from the steel mills lighting a thin
silhouette. Everything was better
in Pittsburgh, even the fog.

How much Christmas dinner must have cost
for a wooing steelworker seeking your hand
and taking you for a night on the town:
he selected boiled Kennebec salmon à la trianon,
but first the olives and young onions
with salted almonds. He reminded you to savor
the sweetbreads glacé à la financière,
while you drank Imperial Punch before
the English plum pudding with mint wafers,
and the Roquefort, Swiss, Neufchatel and tea.

How many games, hands clasped close
with a entrepreneur who played the stocks,
you must have watched
while "The Flying Dutchman"
stole base after base, made hit after hit.

And Schenley Park in the spring!

Amanda Reynolds

On St. Patrick's Day an artist might have
drawn your portrait in chalk, taken you
up Coal Hill to watch the Golden Triangle,
its buildings sinking into the rivers,
the streetcars barely breathing above the flood.

And yet you chose him, loyal to the city,
this man born of Pennsylvania Dutch,
this man for whom you cooked and cleaned,
this man who didn't trust the banks
and kept his money in Braun's
bread bags all over town.
You refused to marry this man
with enough money to own your entire street,
who our family remembers as "Pap"
and who proposed to you time and again.
Another marriage was not something you wanted.
You did want games of Whist,
nights on the couch watching Bruno Sanmartino
wrestle the world, lunches
at 8 p.m. after he finished his work,
three course meals of pork and sauerkraut,
potatoes, and coconut cream pies.
This man found his way into your heart.

THE BANANA EXPLOSION OF 1936

No one believed it at first,
that bananas could bend
the domes of St. Stanislaus,
God's work. Yet for a block,
the glass crashed into the streets.
There was nothing left to do
but drink. "The drinkingest town
 in the west" had a pub
on every street. Long days spent
at Agnew and Brown's
pigeon ball factory earned
small pay, and at James Jelly's
cotton factory they knew
that a draft from a Bakewell's glass
was the way to cut grime
from the throat. Prohibition
wetted these streets
where booze barons worked
as celebrities and whiskey
came at sixteen dollars a quart.
The first club, The Devil's Cave,
sold bourbon in a heavy glass
raised to FDR, the first Democrat
a city like ours could support.
Work in the mills went on
as long as there was beer.
Lights, coal fires, and pitch pots
burned as strong at noon
as in the night. But for every drink
they bent a knee under

Amanda Reynolds

the new stained glass
of St. Stanislaus. Even when
there was no work.
These laws came to the city first.
The gas explosion in the ripening room
twisted towers beyond
what work faith could repair.
So with glass and steel
they rebuilt with pious hearts and drink.

THE BRIDGE OF SIGHS

I'm standing halfway between
the Allegheny Courthouse and the Country Jail,
and this is not Italy.
It's the kind of cold Pittsburgh night
that we endure when everything is melting
and the ugly shows up from underneath.
Still, the bridge has the same name.

The text message you sent
said something about marriage,
so I'm assuming she's finally worn you down.
If this were Venice's *Ponte dei Sospiri*
I'd look down into the *Rio di Palazzo*
for your face. Our kisses long ago
were not always gondola sweet,
but there were sunsets and a promise.

Perhaps love here is different.
This is a city where you can take your prom date
to the morgue, into the chapel to see bodies
in the display case, look in the coolers for familiar
faces. Staring down onto Grant Street
I remember things, like you running faster than me
in the marathon, even with pneumonia.
You were an unbreakable stone,
but at mile ten just past the street
with a lively polka and beer
I saw another man lie down in the street
like a sunning cat and later heard the sirens.

I don't want to turn back,
but ahead only a cool granite cell awaits.

Amanda Reynolds

IF THIS IS THE END

I used to dream of my parents in the front
　　　　seat of the car, not listening when
I told them we were lost, lost beyond directions
　　　　and lost beyond turning back.
Down the concrete boat ramp and into water
　　　　we'd splash at full speed before I awoke.
But this was only a dream after all.
　　　　Even delusions that happen time after time
don't always amount to anything: Grandma digging
　　　　dirt from Hazelwood and slogging it to
Lonaconing, Maryland year after year
　　　　to fill in her mother's grave that kept sinking.
Once, in the '60s a young chemistry major
　　　　from the university drove his '59 Chrysler
off the Bridge to Nowhere, onto the north shore
　　　　of the Allegheny. Without a scratch, he conquered
the unfinished double-deck steel bowstring arch
　　　　and lived to deny all media requests.
The ironworkers, ropes optional, climb the rivets
　　　　hand and foot attacking with hellhounds the heads
of the old salt-soaked metal. A KDKA cameraman climbs
　　　　the fish belly trusses to keep another soul
from jumping. Glenn practices the divine trumpet
　　　　beneath Fort Duquesne bridge where the acoustics
are the best in the city. In the dream, there were no signs
　　　　pointing wrong way, stop, turn back.
If this is the end, give me a sweet ride, big city blues,
　　　　and money to pay the one penny toll.

III.

YELLOW BELT

Call me a glutton.
I still want it all.
I'm pushing car
after car toward
the center
of the city.
I never tried to resist
a single piece of you.
At the Hulton Bridge
I remember finding
you half way
across a river,
running toward
the hospital,
toward your brother
with his brain swollen
from the accident.
I followed you in.
You held me close
for just a moment
before fallen angels
shut me out.

BASEBALL IN THE CITY

No Pittsburgh Pirate
ever hit a ball
out of Yankee Stadium,
but our Josh Gibson did.
That home run king
hit so hard in '32,
the ball left Pittsburgh
and landed in
an outfielder's glove
the next day in Philly.
"You're out,"
yelled the ump.
"You're out,
yesterday,
in Pittsburgh,"
I heard him shout.

And whether I played
the Homestead Grays
or Greenlee's Crawford
Colored Giants,
it was sweet
under the portable lights
on Forbes Field in spring.
Nine pennants. What team
will ever top it?

Every rich kid had a jersey
and every poor woman
on the Hill wore a smart hat

Amanda Reynolds

for weekend games.
They came to watch
Vicious Vic throw those
fists and Chet Brewer
toe the rubber.

When it was over,
sure, I was happy to see
Jackie take the mound,
but I'd play it all away
to see Cool Papa Bell
again, see him running,
running like he stole something.

A WOMAN IS WORTH TWICE
THAT OF A MAN

if she is murdered. She makes
bread, tans hides, shapes clay pots,
dresses game, gathers, fetches, plows,
plants, grinds, and keeps the fire burning.

There's little left of the *Lenni Lenape* here
between the rivers: a plaque, ancestor,
or trail that's lasted hundreds of years.
That branch of my family tree is bare.

This poem is worth twice that of a man.
I can say that since he'll never read it.
He's busy hunting, playing, or ignoring
what I'm doing. Maybe getting shot.

I would sew this story in a belt with beads,
but I'm sure that's out of style.
I've tattooed what gossip I can on my body,
and that didn't attract you either.

This view is worth twice that of your word.
The steel scraped into a gray sky,
never moves or leaves, and I search for how
to touch it all. You slip through my fingers.

The Indians' wolf-like dog is now extinct,
but at night I hear the howling.
Wind? My own voice? A woman hearing
the turtle rattle far away and knowing?

Amanda Reynolds

This night is worth twice that of a life.
The French brought beauty but the English
metal. You bring all but what matters,
and I pound the floor like corn and mortar.

I'm not giving up, but you're so cold.
The city's shouldering up to the moon,
and I still hope to trade for better goods.
The feel of a pearl. A shiny stone.

Stories are worth more than any truth.
This I can handle, and I can pass on.
Do you know that the women conceived
of agriculture first? The Corn Mother tells it.
What I wouldn't give for a medicine bundle:
roots, feathers, a stone, an animal tooth.
My guardian spirit lives in the city
but is never home when I come calling.

One woman is worth more than any horse.
To feed her this man gave his mount for
"as much corn as filled the crown of his hat,"
returning to her on foot and carrying a saddle.

Would you exchange anything for me?
Would I barter one night of flawless stars
for days of blood on my feathers?
Watch me. I'll stoke these flames till the end.

KURT VONNEGUT FLUNKED THERMODYNAMICS AT CARNEGIE TECH

Didn't he study? Didn't he care?
Did he wonder if he'd ever find
a new forte? Decades later another scholar
realized some majors are too demanding,
and switched to bagpipes.
He took his diploma and ran,
full of knowledge of swan-necked bags
and feather bonnets. Still today when
I hear the college fight song
while waiting on hold, it threatens
to make me run screeching.

It wasn't the first paradox of the city.
Earlier and across town,
Henry Frick ordered an elaborate shower
built to his precise corporal specifications,
thousands of dollars of copper pipes,
and dozens of nozzles, each labeled
by body part to massage from his spine
to his liver to his toes. All this, while
outside his mansion more people
died from influenza than the war.

Still people here don't realize
when they're missing the obvious.
Nine buffalo roam South Park,
where there's enough grass for a lifetime,
but enough homeless in the streets
of Pittsburgh that nine buffalo
would only be a snack.

Amanda Reynolds

Do you understand the movement
of energy? Some of us have got it,
and some just don't.
With so many people here,
there are bound to be a few
who don't get it right the first time,
or sometimes never.
I'm with Kurt on this one.
Who cares about a final exam
in transport phenomena in a slaughterhouse?
Or thermodynamic potential
when daily life supplies enough horror
for another chapter? Who cares
of black holes when all you can wash away
the irony and a few sins?
What's a humanist to do in such a city?

TEARING DOWN THE "IGLOO"

It's named Mellon Arena now,
but only broadcasters have to call it that.
Resting on an icy hill, the inverted silver bowl
with a retractable dome has globed
the city's hockey team since 1967.

It's summer forty-one years later now,
and at the groundbreaking for a new arena
I'm breathing 2 feet away from Mario Lemieux.
As godlike as ever he adjusts his shades
and signs a few photos as he glides through.

I've skipped out on work, like so many others
to listen to Jeff Jimmerson sing the anthem
and see the mayor toss up a shovel of dirt
while *Let's go Pens! Let's go Pens!* echoes
off bulldozers and nearby buildings.

At my first game, Dad's friend, Howie, made me
listen to the radio broadcast on my Walkman.
He said I wouldn't understand, but from the puck
drop, I did. When Jagr tucked in his shirt and skated
off, mullet flying in the wind, I was addicted.

I waited for hours for Marty Straka who signed
my jersey upside down, chatted up Wregget
in his alligator loafers, and booed the Flyers loud.
I saved Mario trading cards in Bun candy bars
and tried to skip school for the victory parade.

Amanda Reynolds

Mom remembers when games were cheap,
and the team rarely won, but they sure could fight.
Back then the arena had a real penguin, Pete,
who appeared before games. He died after only
months, but his replacement, Re-Pete, skated on.

We all know Lange and the old 2-9er
get drunk together when there's no game,
Errey's funnier when he's between the benches,
and Malkin has to hit the trainer with the puck
on his way off the ice. Jeff Reed sits in section C.

Big Ben hangs out in Lemieux's box,
and every day's a great day for hockey here.
You should duck when the cotton candy man goes by,
and boo louder when Hossa comes to town.
A Kasparaitis jersey is still a safe bet for now.

Save me a seat in that new arena please,
though I can't promise I'll love it quite as much.
At least Briere and number 66 will still have banners
in the eves, and the organ will echo from above.
Half the reason I came back is hockey, maybe more.

IV.

GREEN BELT

Like the lustful blown about
in a squall, I dodge
        traffic cones and ideas,
but they keep coming.
Every time I think it's the last turn,
there's another bridge to cross.

        It's February, but lukewarm,
which is an awful taunt
with so many more bitter weeks
to go. Once, someone asked
me to write a self-portrait;
I became a palm tree with icicles,
        glittering and fragile
like the rivers that thaw and waver
under the South Highland Bridge.

I want to stop for a picture,
but there's no room, no time,
        no guardrail.
The sidewalk just lets go into
traffic. The kids at the crosswalk
get loose for a moment to shrug
        or sniffle, knowing
a hand will still be there.
The lights change and set free
the traffic ahead of me.

When spring comes, Kennywood,
        bumper cars and all,

will reopen, and concerts will blare
at Hartwood Acres while the gardeners
will again have work in Fox Chapel.

You tricked me for just a moment,
          melted me enough
to blow free. I unraveled
what was left of hope and swung
out that limb when we stayed out late
one fall evening after I had come home,
and you held my face in your hands.

Here I am again though, driving
          and free
to move on. Still I'm looping
my little world for a way out.

The sign where the green belt ends
has been stolen, so I stagger on
through stoplights for a while
before twisting back toward the start.
It's hard to give up the chase,
even though I know it's long gone.
When I surrender, I'm rewarded
for just a moment with a glimpse
through all the traffic and glare.
          I can see ahead
as far as this highway goes,
straight to the city's heart.

Amanda Reynolds

DEAR GRANDMA

I guess you endured.
Waited calm
like Chief Shannopin
for the white men to come.
Waited for your movie star
husband's postcards.
He wrote to you:
This is a good picture of the plane
I tried to fly. Remember, dear,
I told you about how I pre-flighted
that P-40 down in the woods?
I got this for the scrapbook
so we could recall that.
Boy was it a close one.
You persisted
like General Braddock
at Fort Duquesne who understood:
We shall know better how to deal with them
another time.
Did you learn to sew,
cook, clean, and play the piano
that you left to a neighbor
when you died?
Your husband showed you
the world: *These men look just like*
we looked yesterday.
They are firing from a kneeling position.
The targets are right along the seashore,
and we fire out toward the sea.
You should see the splash

when the bullets hit the water.
The fellows standing just behind
the men firing are on the "ready line"
and will fire next.
As high as 4000 men have fired
on our range in one day.
You waited
like John Boyd hanging on the hill
to punish an unfaithful wife.
Like Henry Heinz
on his tiny horseradish plant
for the big day to come.
Like the Hunkies
on the boat.
Like the Homestead Grays
waiting to bat.
So young the bride,
how poor you must have been
at waiting for anything.

Amanda Reynolds

WHAT THE TRAIN SAYS

From my house
        on the
   hill
        I hear honey,
chai, cinnamon, like swirls
        through
   the valley.

Near the
               river
        it yowls
             hollow.

And from far
   or not so far
             a cruel
   silver city
never
        fails to
        whisper back.

WHAT THE MEN SAY

Dear Mother, I earned my Quarterly Conference
license for the United Brethren today.
I wish father could see the church: strong pews,
strong souls. The men shook my hand,
and the women made pies with peaches
they carried from Coal Bank Hollow Road.
They were too sweet, but with strong coffee
I suppose I'll manage. Next month we leave
on the circuit. I have chosen a bay mare
to carry my saddlebags. My passport through
the Southern lines should arrive any day.
Be strong—war is inevitable.
Give my best to the folks,
Rev. William A. Jackson, 1862.

Sons, our clan now has no chief, but once,
once, we ruled Scotland. Carnegie is a poor
Scotch immigrant like us. What can you not find
in Pittsburgh? There's Orkney cheese at the deli
and Arbroath smokies at Macbain's.
Beware the "water of life." Black Douglas drank
too deep of life and too often.
It was the English who called him "Black."
For us, he can always be the Good Sir James—
Douglas! Douglas! he cried that Palm Sunday
when he captured the English prisoners, beheaded
them, left them to burn. God forgive weakness
in men. When I am long gone, you boys battle.
R. Stewart, Pittsburgh, 1910.

Amanda Reynolds

Hello folks: I went through
classification this morning, and I'm in.
They say stenographer and seem to be saving
me for something. Most of the gang
is gone or going this morning.
I think we'll move to the day house
to make room for foreign service men
who've made it back. Love, Ted, 1941.

I'm going, hon. It looks like I will be even farther
now, but it also looks good. Love, Ted, 1941.

Dear Peg, Here is some Mexican jewelry.
I was always sorry I did not get some when
I was there, but at last here is a pin I thought
you would like. I got it in a shop in Hollywood, hon.
It is from Mexico, though.
The target was rapid fire honey,
and I had the feel of the gun a little better.
My score was seventy-two
out of 100, which would qualify.
All my love dear, Ted, 1944.

Good news. Last week there was a near miss.
I hope you have been receiving my telegrams.
We were sent over the Rhine on a mission.
But today!
The Yanks have crossed the Remagen Bridge.
It was that same bridge we missed. My love, Ted, 1945.

WHAT THE WOMEN SAY

Dear Friend, I've not heard from you in so long
I wondered if you were sick. I presume
you are doing the "Good Samaritan"
for children, as usual. If it is convenient
for you to have me come, I would be very glad
to see you. I am of course busy,
but I expect to always be so—
I might as well take the time—
there is no prospect of a dull season as I can see.
I do wish everyone was busy—
the World would be running
smooth. I am sorry to see so many unemployed—
hope the President will arrange for all to be employed.
I am only sending a line to ask if you are well. Please
let me know before Saturday
if I should come as I leave here for Pittsburg
that day. Yours, Pauline, 1921.

Dear Edward, the evening of your
birthday I stop to remember.
The church misses you most of all.
The boarding house on Tullymet Street,
near the Hill, reminds me of Sunday school,
how shy you were at our first picnic.
When father built our house in Hazelwood
and Edward, William, and Grace came along,
how did I know that these mills and mines
could ever take you away? Hay fever!
In these thirty years, I have missed
mountains of your red hot coal.
Sarah Ethel Hill, Allegheny, 1942.

Dear Karen, You should know about
my great grandmother, Jean Douglas,
who married Grandfather Love.
Her funeral procession drove in carriages
and wagons to the cemetery
way up on Detmold Mtn.
Here, we picked wild pansies
and dug a bit of sassafras.
Patton Mine nearby
was small. The families were large.
We emigrated from Scotland
and found Lonaconing—
Uncle Douglas Love was shot to death.
They say the Molly Maguires did it,
but I have never seen proof.
From Lonaconing we'd ride the old C&P RR
near Mount Savage where hills were so high
the train climbed up so far,
then backed up so far,
then climbed again, chewing up the mountain.
You never went to Cumberland and back
in one day, because what you found there was
Grandma Harper's porch, too high
and oh so close to heaven—
We came back to Pittsburgh.
There's no future in Maryland for a girl.
Marion J. Muirhead, age 92, 1986.

V.

BLUE BELT

Lasciate ogne speranza, voi ch'intrate

My new distraction lives
right off the blue belt,
and on a first date
we drove some of the circle
looking at the mansions
and manors—
when the music
of Stephen Foster
filled halls and Mary Croghan,
scandalized the city,
leaving boarding school
in Long Island and eloping
to England with 43-year-old
Captain Edward Schenley.
The lovely park that bears
her name is near your home.

There's no traffic this late
on the Blue Belt,
where I'm driving again.
My mind wanders
at a red light, but only a few weeks
back. This is progress.
Kiss me like you want me.
I want you to write a poem
about this, he breathed in my ear.
I want to stop at his apartment
as I drive by so close, but I'm
not sure he's what I want yet.

I try hard to keep his voice
in my ear, the feel of his arms
around my shoulders
—*I have to have you*—
but I'm still thinking
of other crazy things
I've done for love. I miss the turn
near Boyd's Hill and circle back,
making the same mistake twice.

Can this be anywhere near the center
of the earth? The way out of it all?
Can a new love absolve me?
As I turn the car away toward home,
the last look I take is at the stars.

Amanda Reynolds

HEINZ 56

Seems like I've been cooking
gnocchi and manicotti ever since
I asked Mom about the family tree.
You're Heinz 56, she said.
Everything but Italian.
That time I picked
the most interesting
dish to bring to class: corn bread
for the Shawnee Indians
of the Ohio River Valley.

Now, sauce, rich with my parents'
homemade Valpolicella,
simmers on the stove all afternoon
in my steel worker kitchen.
Grandma makes the noodles from scratch,
and pizzelles are Dad's favorite
Christmas treat.

They're fitting contradictions.
What does the 57 in that ketchup
stand for anyway?
The number of ingredients? No.
The year of creation? No.
It's John Heinz's lucky number, five,
and his wife's auspicious digit, seven.
Nothing special. Two ingredients.
Five and seven. Pasta and sauce.

THE SHAPE OF A CITY

Two funiculars
remain inclined
on Mt. Washington.
On the ride up,
"The Golden Triangle"
becomes a tiny
platter of glass and steel.
And riding down
is like a heavy coal
centering in my gut.

I know the gumwood
and locust rollers
are long gone,
and that cast-iron sheaves
pull us up and down—
arms and eyes—
legs and ears.
What is friction?

Kirk Lewis be damned.
Your incline you made
hoists my head in and out
of a latitudinal groove.
Alarm: 1 Bell. Ready:
2 Bells. Start: 3 Bells.
No foul language.
No credits for freight.

Amanda Reynolds

Do not open the
rectangular panic button
(aka the window).
The Tin Angel watches
down from the heights,
and at another restaurant
nearby, over dinner,
Dad proposed marriage,
and ever since I've been
crashing down the cables,
further from this city.

LOOKING DOWN ON THE SOUTH SIDE
FROM MY NEW HOME

The steel mills
are replaced
by dull monstrosities,
restaurants and bars
all Art Deco,
pastel, manufacturing
"forbidden fruit"
drinks. Progress
in this city
takes the scraps,
and makes sweet
grimy ingots,
slabs, and sheet—
everything the same,
shiny aluminum
with tedious iron links.

The diners are restless.
They smoke, smoke,
and generate
industry with
forged grins.
When my grandfather
retired, Jones
and Laughlin Steel
lined the rivers
with barges
and banners,
great hope

Amanda Reynolds

for years to come.
From deadly
factory to the next
big fashion trend,
there's always
new work
to do here;
but molten world,
we're all being
rolled into one.

THE GREAT PITTSBURGH FIRE (1845)

The Irish washerwoman wandered away from the kettle's
flame to get clothes, and with several week without rain
it didn't take long for embers to waft and settle
on the roof of her hut. The reservoir empty from the strain

of sun and drought, no water came from the hand-pumped
engine. The flare that began at Second and Ferry soon became
the burn that took Colonel Diehl's house and jumped
right through the cotton factory's doors to take aim

at the Third Presbyterian Church. When the cornice caught
fire, the men chopped off the steeple to save the building,
while "all the salt of Sodom" in wagons and carts was brought
to keep the warehouses of coffee and sugar from flaming.

It's said that Mrs. Maglone was one of only two who died
along with Samuel who went back for the piano he left inside.

Amanda Reynolds

LOVE POEM ON A SNOWY DAY

I was attracted to you from the moment I saw you,
like the bridges that glow Aztec gold in the morning sun.

I don't want it to end. The rivers are frozen hard
but flow all the way to the Gulf if you have patience.

I could kiss your cheeks all night long. Soft and smooth
as the houses look in fog, clinging and crawling up the hills.

How do you want me? The way the old air beacon blinks
without pause. Dot dash dash dot, spelling the city's name.

I live for this like that underground fire that's burned thirty
years and sends smoke and flames licking at the headstones.

Let's do this all day. The city will be there tomorrow.
Even Sandburg waited it out ten days in a Pittsburgh jail.

I want you. The way the snow enfolds the sharp edges
of the skyline, bonds to steel, softens and covers all.

LOVE POEM IN SPRING

I knew better.
How many times have I said,
nothing good comes from
Ohio? Now, the dawn
in the river looks like
tarnished gold
leaching into mud
along the shore.
It's only a matter of time
for the houses all aching
and tired, to release
their grips on the cliffs.
The skyscrapers hide below
the heavy fog.
I rarely think of you,
not even of a clean
snowy day when we stayed
in bed and I understood
the whole world.
You are an abandoned city,
Detroit, or Cleveland,
my big mistake.

Amanda Reynolds

THE OLDE SALT RESTAURANT

for Rege and Nancy

I'd come in, prop my head up
on the trusty counter,
and shape sausages
into the usual trees or stars.
I'd carefully butter the toast
to the edges, as ordered.
The mornings were expected and fine.
A tap on the shoulder
from behind or a white face
in a high window only appeared
after closing time.
The three dining rooms
had too many antiques with too much dust,
and on one wall a red line
marked the flood waters from the river
gone off course. Amongst the pictures,
the railroad signals and switches,
the antique coffee cans and maps,
a flash of light sometimes appeared
or a noise in an empty corner.
It wasn't such a bad choice for them.
The innocent ghosts watched me trip and spill
drinks, giggled when the Wilsons
left me only pennies,
and turned the vacuum on and off
late at night. The women's restroom
had a trickster who liked to lock the door,
and a little boy cried behind the wooden
rocking horse. Two gunslingers

tossed fists behind a wooden bar.
But the ones who scared me
the most, were those I never saw
and the story I already knew.
They tap-tapped on the kitchen floor
from the basement, the slave
and her children, and wherever safety was,
they never found it.

Amanda Reynolds

VI.

PURPLE BELT

Fraud. Cheat. Phony.
Swindler since 1995.
So, that's where I left him.
Right on Penn Avenue
with a suitcase, squealing
like a lunatic at my fading
Jeep taillights.

Unlike the other belts,
this wine colored
path doesn't help you
go anywhere,
except into traffic.
It's only for tourists,
googley-eyed lovestruck
out-of-towners
who are seeking the sites
but don't understand
why Pittsburghers wait
patiently for traffic
to make an illegal
left at a red light.

Heading for the stars
is foolish. I went straight
over the rivers
toward home.
I was happy to be off
his track. Free to pick
up a real lover,
to take my city back.

VEGETABLE WARS

I awoke this morning to zucchini carnage
flung about the backyard. The dog pranced
and swaggered, squash guts oozing from her teeth.

Biodegradable ravages. Spoils of salad.
Wasted young and delicate, no fritters,
no sautéing, no baking, no soup.

The neighbor, herbaceous conqueror,
had earlier traversed the risky alley
to place the vegetable atop my rusty garbage can.

And so I had to offer a similar gesture of peace.
What type of gift for this 50-year resident
of a shabby fortress? Wine? Chocolate?

My gallant canine? No. There must be bread.
Pumpkin, walnut, sweet, sweet bread.
Kill them with kindness I must! Put this to an end.

But tomatoes kept coming, one after the other.
And peppers, and onions, and bags of ripe squash.
I became a right hermit avoiding the loot.

A few days later, armed with hot pepper mix,
I was ready to cross the line again. But in return
was fresh salsa, cookies, and homemade pizzelles.

So, with heavy heart and a full kitchen shelf,
I admit defeat. I can't win the vegetable war,
so thank god for a Pittsburgh winter.

Amanda Reynolds

IROQUOIS TRADITION

On a long ride
at the forks
of the Susquehanna,
Shickellamy revealed
to his companion
that he dreamed
last night
of the excellent
rifle Weiser
would provide
him with,
and so as etiquette
demanded,
it was so.

Weiser dreamed
that next night
of the island
in the river
that Shickellamy
would give him,
and by sunset
he was fishing there.

For the future,
and the security
of their friendship
Weiser and Shickellamy
agreed never to
dream together again.

MT. OLIVER

Years ago in my neighborhood
John Cameron grew pumpkins
big enough for the ball,
peas for the princess,
donkey cabbages and sweet squash
like diamonds in the rough.
But for every fairy tale a villain.
When General Jackson came to call,
Cameron refused his vegetable plea.
No work for Pittsburgh on the Sabbath.

My new home's a bit like this, with registers
that clank and toll the midnight hour
and a grinning yellow cat who purrs
upon the porch and just as quickly disappears.

Oliver Ormsby's left gremlins
in this land. Just imagine the hogs, dogs,
and rats all big enough to chase little boys
and they swinging a hickory branches
like baseball bats. Not much is new.
Ask the ogre, the tire-slasher,
the ski-masked pizza hold-up man.
Ask the raven, the cabbie-shooter,
or my quiet neighbor up the hill.

As long as I'm safe inside, I watch
the houses along the hill I face
like square confections, sugary, pastel blue,
lemon chiffon, sweet reflections,

Amanda Reynolds

cherry red. They line up for my choosing,
each wearing a perfect suit, brick-laced,
porch-frosted, sweet and tall.
Tonight, beaten and whipped by the rain
each winks back at me with lights like
glints from swords of many valiant knights.

GHOST CITY

Someone in my family died in a Chinese restaurant,
"drunk" and from "falling down the stairs."
It's what the death certificate reads.
In the same box waits a copy of King James
pressing a piece of silk from Roosevelt's coffin.
There are funeral cards, a woman's lace,
and cracking four leaf clovers. I wonder where
in this city a man could have found Chinese
amongst deli sandwiches from Donahoe's
and cherry pastries from Jenny Lee's.
But *anything can happen,*
says our "Dr. General" Jackson,
the old city barber who each year rides
in the parades on a white charger.
I was in Mexico, he claims. *I fought in the Civil War!*
There are others in my family I never met
who must rest uneasy, like Uncle Chuck
who ran over Aunt Lucy, breaking her leg.
I've even heard that there are those who die
in this city right there in the bar with another
touchdown. And sometimes when there isn't.
Let's meet under the Kaufmann's clock one last time
if you go before I do. We'll share a meal
at the Tic Toc Shop and take peanut brittle for the ride.
I'll tell you the story of how working
as a cocktail waitress on the Gateway Clipper fleet,
we called the riverboats the "Gateway to Hell,"
and when the wind was strong we couldn't dock
at Three Rivers Stadium. The drunks leaned overboard,
and I waited for the splash. But, what right
have I to judge? My own family gave away Uncle Dink
to neighbors because of too many mouths to feed.

Amanda Reynolds

EVERYTHING AND NOTHING

When I call my friend
to complain about all my
misfortunes, she offers
a simple solution: you were
a dreadful person
in another life.
It's so matter of fact,
but now I'm thinking
I should have told her:

It's possible.
I might have been
Queen Aliquippa
sipping Chinese ginseng
and flirting with the general
no one knew yet,
George Washington.
So today I'm doomed
to pay for my feathered
eyebrows with eons of men
who turn into flesh-eating
forest beasts at the sound
of the word "stay"
(they're a little soft
around the middle
but have horns and claws
beneath the fur).

I suppose it could be true
that I was the scab,

the strikebreaker,
the first shot at the riot.
When Dickens called my city
an ugly confusion of backs
of buildings and crazy
galleries and stairs,
I might have spit in his eye
and loved Pittsburgh
for all the dark places.
Perhaps that's why I could never
be the skinny red-headed Italian
he wished for on Valentine's Day.

And maybe I was John Boyd's
unfaithful wife expecting my husband
to kill my lover and save my honor.
That could be why still today I can't forget
my first love who calls once a year
to remind me of our long-gone anniversary.
I was never enough,
you will always love me,
and all that star-crossed lovers propaganda.

I was the one who lit the match.
I was the slumlord of the shantytown,
the snake in Franklin's cartoon,
the English driving
Chief Pontiac into the ground,
the fog and smoke that made the city
look like night at noon.

Amanda Reynolds

I was the wealthy,
eating off the glass plates
that someone chopped his fingers off
to make. I was cholera and pitch pots in the street.
Everything and nothing,
I am the whiskey that burns your throat.

NOTES

WISHING YOU WERE HERE

Isaly's is a popular deli chain, famous for its "chipped ham," that has been in Pittsburgh since the early 1900's.

A second baseman during the 1880's and 1890's, Louis Bierbauer actually played for the Philadelphia Athletics before becoming an outlaw in the Players' League that formed in 1890. When that league folded after a year, the Athletics, for whatever reason, left Bierbauer off the roster of players to reincorporate into their team. Seizing the opportunity, the Pittsburgh team "pirated" him for their own, earning the name that has stuck since.

THE MOLLY MAGUIRES

True evidence of the Molly Maguires in America is questionable, although there is record of their existence as a secret Irish organization. The group was blamed for crimes during mid-19th century in the coalfields of the U.S., but most evidence was provided by industrialists and owners who it is suggested were hiding their own misdeeds.

WHAT WE WERE EATING

The last goalie to face a puck in Pittsburgh without a mask was Andy Brown on April 7, 1974.

Sidney Crosby is/was the captain of the Pittsburgh Penguins.

WAR SCENES

"No bluebirds at the cliffs of Dover" refers to a song "There'll be Bluebirds over the White Cliffs of Dover," which was made popular by Vera Lynn during WWII. Ironically, there are no bluebirds found in Britain.

J&L is short for Jones and Laughlin, a steel company in Pittsburgh.

"Glimmering and vast" references Matthew Arnold's poem "Dover Beach."

WHAT A CHOICE MEANS
Thanks to Stephen Lorant, who wrote *Pittsburgh: The Story of an American City*, for his insightful description and memorable images of the city's fog.

"The Flying Dutchman" is Honus Wagner, a famous shortstop who played for the Pittsburgh Pirates. He was one of the first five players inducted into the Baseball Hall of Fame in 1936 with votes just behind Ty Cobb and tied with Babe Ruth.

Bruno Sanmartino is the longest-running champion of the World Wide Wrestling Foundation.

THE BANANA EXPLOSION OF 1936
In 1936, a gas explosion occurred in the ripening room of the Pittsburgh Banana Company's building. The explosion bent the domes and shattered the windows of a nearby church, St. Stanislaus.

IF THIS IS THE END
"The Bridge to Nowhere" refers to the Fort Duquesne Bridge that was constructed 1958-63. Because of a lack of funding, the bridge did not span the river and open to traffic until 1969.

BASEBALL IN THE CITY
Josh Gibson was an American catcher who played for the Homestead Grays, the Pittsburgh Crawfords, Ciudad Trujillo, and the Mexican League from 1930-41. Although he was unable to play in Major League Baseball because of his race, he was

elected to the Baseball Hall of Fame in 1972 and is considered one of the best power hitters to play the game.

The "Hill" refers to the "Hill District," which was once considered the center of African-American culture in Pittsburgh.

Jackie Robinson's break into Major League Baseball also marked the demise of African-American leagues.

"Cool Papa Bell," or James Thomas Bell, was a center fielder for the Pittsburgh Crawfords and the Homestead Grays.

KURT VONNEGUT FLUNKED THERMODYNAMICS
Carnegie Tech, founded by Andrew Carnegie in 1900, was one of the precursors to Carnegie Mellon University.

Henry Frick was an industrialist who earned his fortune in Pittsburgh.

TEARING DOWN THE "IGLOO"
Jeff Jimmerson is a beloved Pittsburgher who more often than not sings the national anthem at Penguins' games.

Jaromir Jagr played for the Penguins from 1990-1994 and 1995-2001 and helped the team to win two Stanley Cups.

"Lange" refers to the Penguins' announcer, Mike Lange.

"The old 2-9er" is Phil Borque, former NHL player and Pittsburgh Penguin who does radio commentary with Mike Lange.

"Errey" refers to Bob Errey, another former player and television announcer.

"Malkin" is Evgeni Malkin, a current Penguins player.

Jeff Reed was a kicker for the Pittsburgh Steelers and member of the 2009 Super Bowl team.

Big Ben refers to Ben Roethlisberger, a quarterback for the Pittsburgh Steelers.

Marian Hossa was traded from the Penguins to the defending Stanley Cup champions, the Detroit Red Wings, in 2008.

Darius Kasparaitis is a tough defenseman who played for the Penguins 1996-2002.

Michel Briere is one of only two players to have his number retired by the Penguins. He was killed in an automobile accident in 1970.

"Number 66" is Mario Lemieux.

DEAR GRANDMA

Chief Shannopin of the Delaware tribe had his village on the southern bank of the Allegheny River.

The italicized text is taken from postcards sent from Edward Jackson (my maternal grandfather) to his wife, Margaret Jackson during WWII.

General Edward Braddock led a British force in the French and Indian War. After his defeat on the banks of the Monongahela, his dying words are reported as: *We shall know better how to deal with them another time.*

"Hunkies" refers to the group of Pittsburghers of Polish, Hungarian, Russian, and Slovak nationalities.

The Homestead Grays were a Pittsburgh area baseball team formed in 1912 that enjoyed success in the Negro Leagues.

WHAT THE MEN IN MY FAMILY HAVE SAID

These "found poems" are letters written by men in my family. They have been changed some, but many of the lines are their original words.

WHAT THE WOMEN IN MY FAMILY HAVE SAID

These "found poems" are letters written by women in my family. They have been changed some, but many of the lines are their original words.

For a brief period of history, "Pittsburgh" was spelled without the "h" mainly due to a clerical error. After protests from the citizens, the "h" was returned to the name in 1911.

BLUE BELT

"*Lasciate ogne speranza, voi ch'intrate*" is the inscription on Dante's gate of hell in the *Inferno*, which can be translated as "Abandon all hope, ye who enter here."

Minos judges those who have committed "active" sins by wrapping his tail around himself a corresponding number of times.

In the *Inferno*, Virgil and Dante ultimately escape hell through the center of the earth and on the dawn of Easter Sunday are greeted by a sky full of stars.

The last word of Dante's *Divine Comedy* in all three sections is "stelle" or stars.

THE SHAPE OF A CITY

The financial district or downtown area of Pittsburgh is often referred to as "The Golden Triangle."

IROQUOIS TRADITION

The Susquehanna is a river near Pittsburgh.

MT. OLIVER

Mt. Oliver is a Pittsburgh neighborhood on the south side of the city.

John Cameron, who was reported to grow the best vegetables in Pittsburgh, refused to sell his produce when Stonewall Jackson came to town because it was a Sunday.

GHOST CITY

Although the department store Kauffman's no longer exists, the famous clock that adorns the corner is still a recognizable feature from the street and a favorite meeting place for Pittsburghers.

EVERYTHING AND NOTHING

Supposedly Queen Aliquippa of the Seneca tribe flirted with General George Washington when he arrived at Pittsburgh.

Charles Dickens visited Pittsburgh in 1842 with his wife. He was not impressed.

Benjamin Franklin's political cartoon in 1754 showed a snake in pieces, which represented the "disunited" colonies in America.

Amanda Reynolds